Trace each numeral. Start on the green dots.

Name

CONTENTS

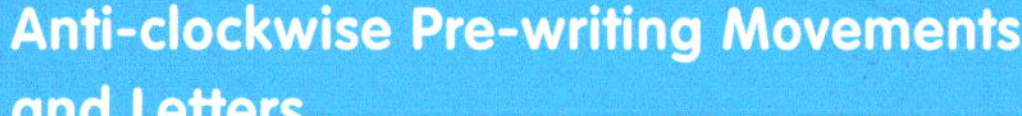

INTRODUCTION

The current Queensland handwriting script was introduced over several years from 1985, after a successful trial. Its print style, the Beginner's Alphabet, is based on simple, italic cursive shapes that are easily joined to become Queensland Modern Cursive. Because capitals remain the same, the two scripts merge easily, so children find cursive writing much easier to write as well as read. Queensland Modern Cursive is designed to be fluent and quick, with maximum legibility.

FOCUS

This book contains an appropriate sequence of handwriting activities for children in their prep year at school:

- the introduction of lower-case letters in recommended rotation groups —straight letters, clockwise letters, anti-clockwise letters and letters with both rotations
- pre-writing patterns for each letter shape are explored through a nursery rhyme theme, including lots of tracing and colouring in
- letters are traced and placed on a blue base line, with a strong emphasis on correct direction and fluency, top-to-bottom and left-to-right movements
- letters are reduced in size to fit on 8 mm Year One red and blue lines, with head, body and tail spatial-awareness markers.
- Theme: nursery rhymes.

TECHNIQUE

Pencil grip

1. The thumb and the index finger support the pencil while it rests on the middle finger.
2. Child should be able to tap the pencil with the pointer finger while it is supported by the middle finger and thumb.
3. There should be a distance of approx. 2–2.5 cm from the pencil point to the tip of the index finger, 3 cm for a left-hander. Triangular pencil-grips promote correct finger placement and distance.

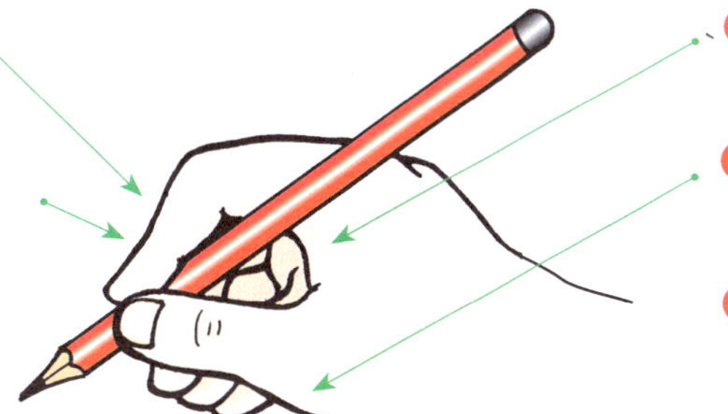

4. Hold pencil barrel up high, near or before the knuckle. Pencil should not rest low in the "web" of the hand.
5. The side of the hand and the little finger act as supports for the whole hand.
6. Unpainted pencils are less slippery.

Posture

Right-handers

1. Keep back straight at an angle of about 30° to back of chair, and keep bottom towards back of seat.
2. Make sure that book or paper is sufficient distance from the edge of the desk to enable most/all of the forearm to rest on the desk. Move book up as child works down the page to maintain this.
3. Table or desk height about level with child's waistline or a bit higher. The weight of the body is supported by the non-writing arm.
4. Sloping desks are ideal, especially for struggling writers.

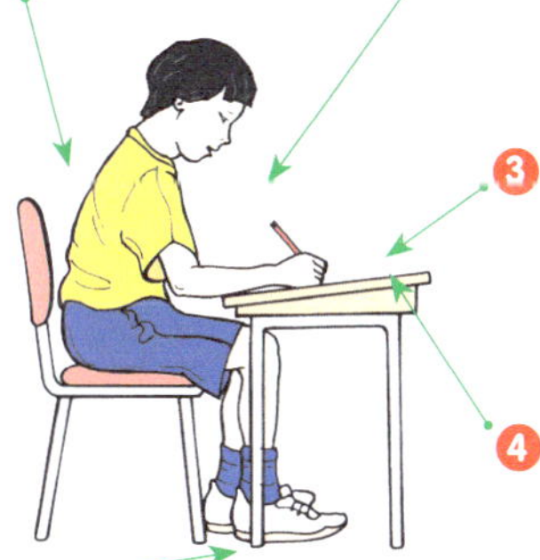

5. Feet should touch the floor (use a telephone book if needed).

Left-handers

Left-handers should have their elbow in to discourage a hooked wrist.

Posture rhyme:

1, 2, 3, 4. Are your feet flat on the floor?
5, 6, 7, 8. Is your back nice and straight?
9, 10, 11, 12. Show me how your pencil's held.
13, 14, 15, 16. Now it's time to do some writing.

GENERAL TEACHING TIPS

- Purchase extra copies of *Write for Queensland*—Prep to laminate for non-permanent marker use, allowing incidental, all-year reinforcement of handwriting lessons.
- Display the alphabet in lower-case and upper-case forms across the top of the board.
- Always commence writing lessons with finger exercises, incorporating rhymes, such as "Twinkle, Twinkle, Little Star", or "One Day My Thumb Was Moving", or games such as finger Olympics, mock piano playing, spider on a mirror, etc.
- Utilise old verbal letter cues to assist with direction, e.g. letter "b" like a bat and a ball: down for the bat and up and around for the ball.
- Modelling on a board or an overhead screen one letter at a time, and writing large letters in the air as a class, assists direction also.
- Slope is developmental and should be encouraged, but not enforced, at this stage.
- Felt pens/textas are ideal for pre-writing. Soft HB pencils (unpainted) are recommended for later stages.

Please see further information on the learning features of this book in the Teacher's Notes on page 47.

l

Trace the strings. Draw more. Start on the green dots.

Old King Cole was a merry old soul,
And a merry old soul was he;
He called for his pipe,
And he called for his bowl,
And he called for his fiddlers three.

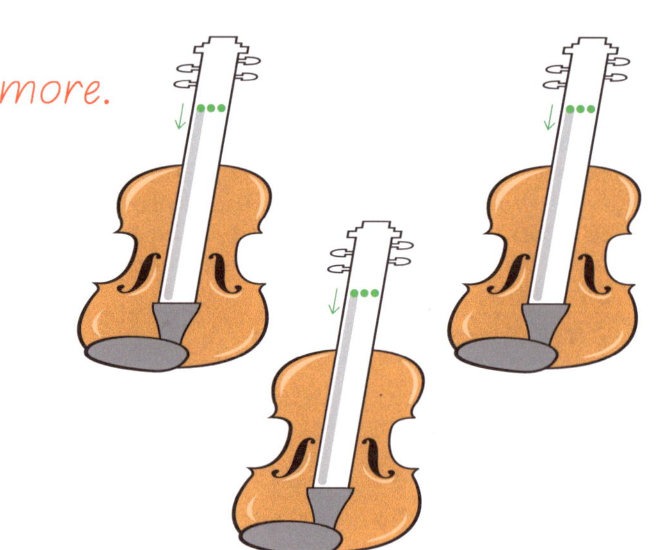

Trace the railings. Draw more.

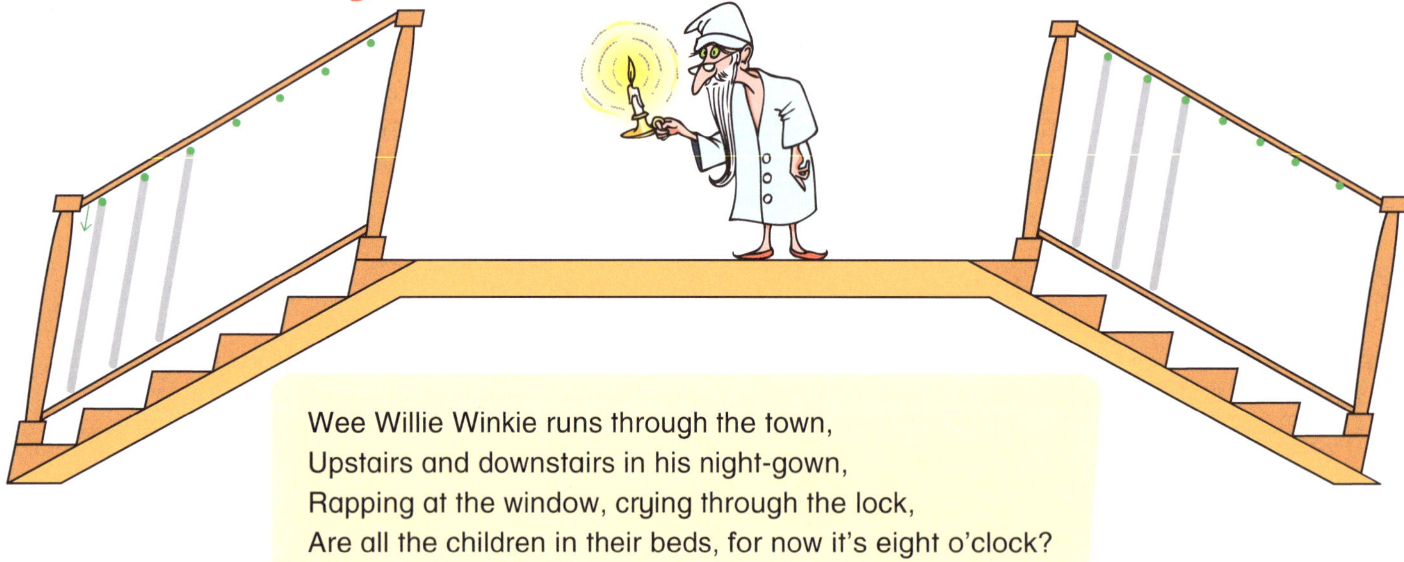

Wee Willie Winkie runs through the town,
Upstairs and downstairs in his night-gown,
Rapping at the window, crying through the lock,
Are all the children in their beds, for now it's eight o'clock?

Trace and write l.

Trace and write l.

Trace the candles. Add flames.
Draw more.

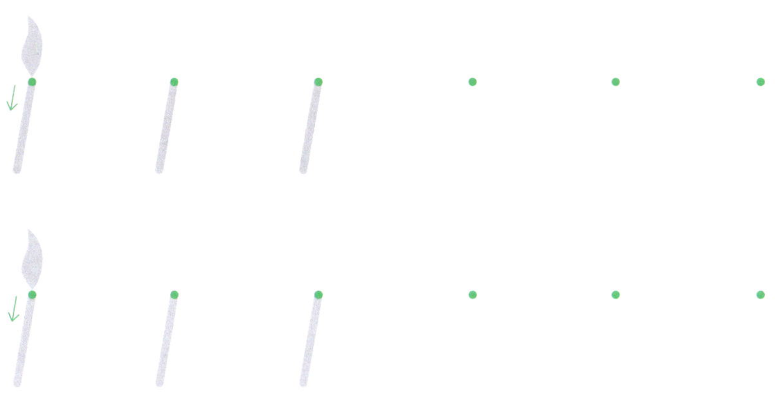

Jack be nimble,
Jack be quick,
Jack jump over
The candlestick.

Trace and write i.

Draw more sultanas. Colour.

Little Jack Horner
Sat in the corner,
Eating his Christmas pie;
He put in his thumb,
And pulled out a plum,
And said, "What a good boy am I!"

Trace and write i.

t

Trace the train track.
Draw more.
Start on the green dots.

Trace the train tracks. Draw more.

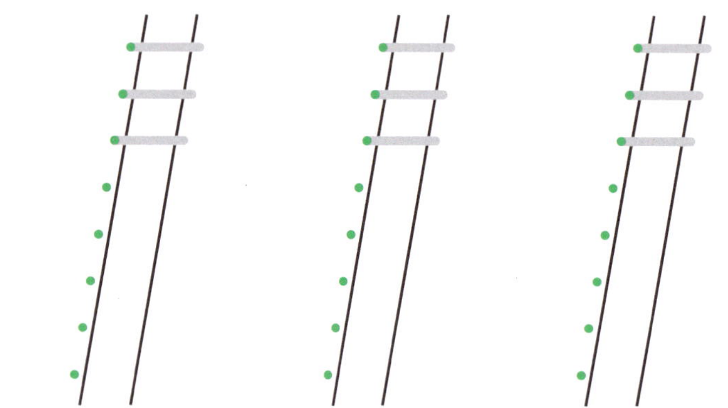

Down by the station,
Early in the morning,
See the little puffer trains
All in a row.
See the engine driver
Turn the little handle,
Chug-chug
Toot-toot
Off we go!

Write t on each hot cross bun. Trace and write t.

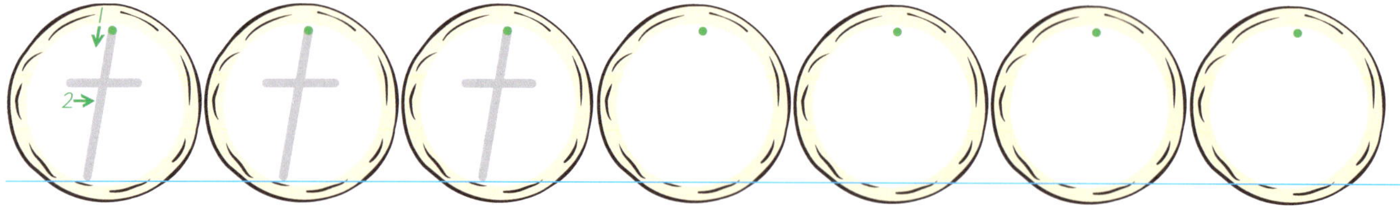

Trace and write t.

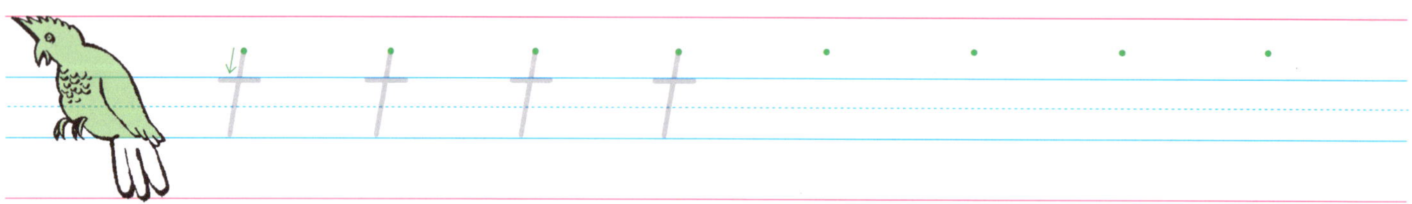

Trace and continue the pattern.

Trace and write x.

Colour.

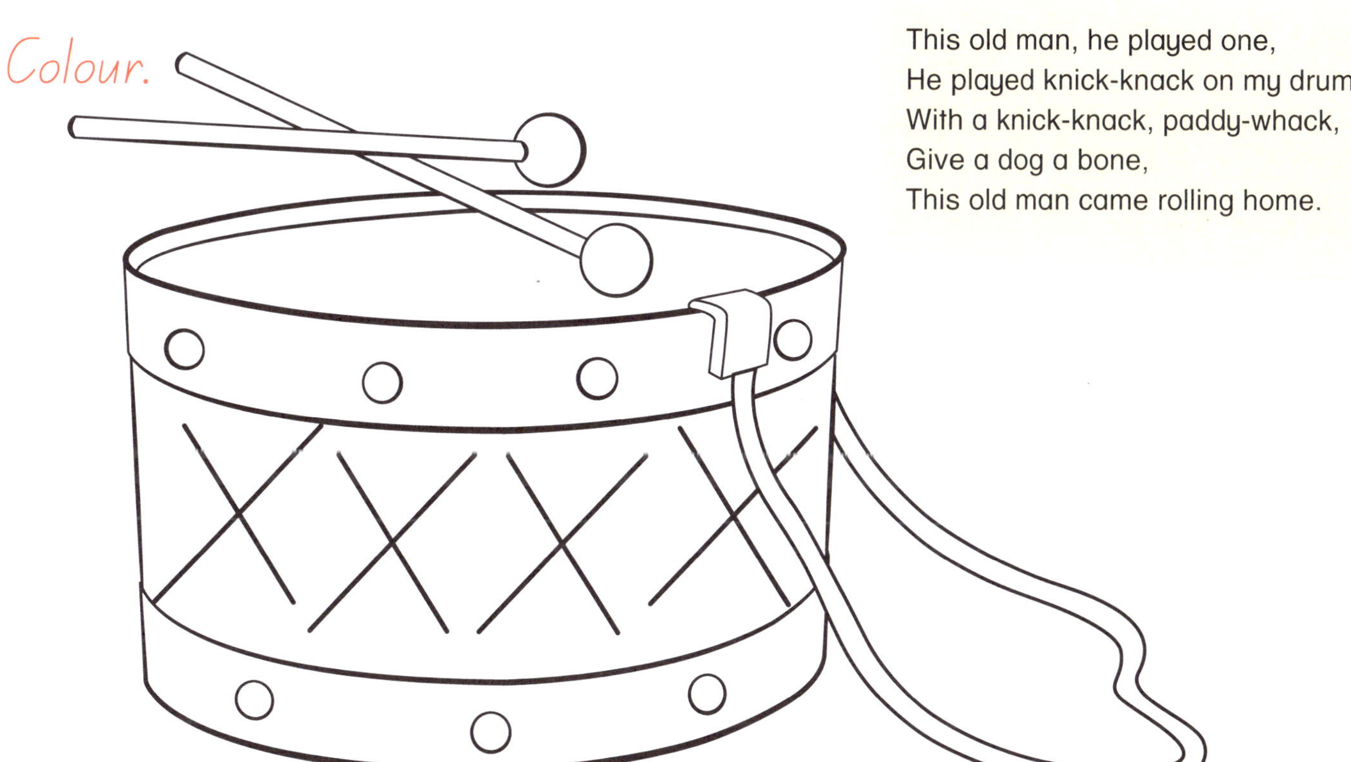

This old man, he played one,
He played knick-knack on my drum.
With a knick-knack, paddy-whack,
Give a dog a bone,
This old man came rolling home.

Trace and write x.

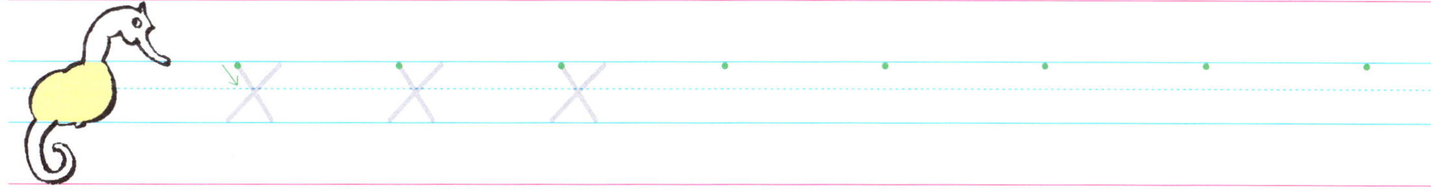

n

Trace to finish the umbrellas.
Start on the green dots.

It's raining, it's pouring,
The old man is snoring.
He bumped his head
on the back of the bed,
And couldn't get up in the morning.

Trace and continue the pattern.

Trace to finish the seashell cockleshells.

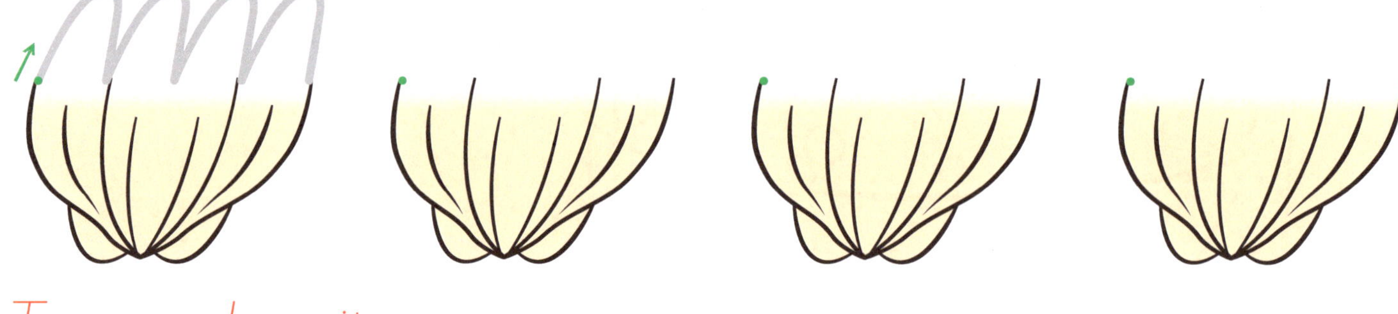

Trace and write n.

Trace and write n.

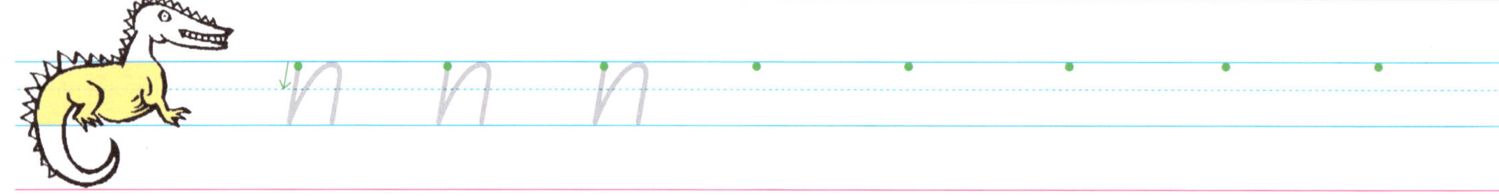

Trace and continue the pattern.

Put handles on Doctor Foster's bags.

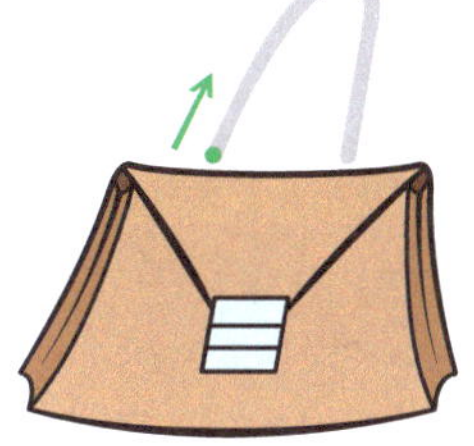

Trace and write n.

Colour. Add rain.

Doctor Foster went to Gloucester
In a shower of rain;
He stepped in a puddle,
Right up to his middle,
And never went there again.

Trace and write n.

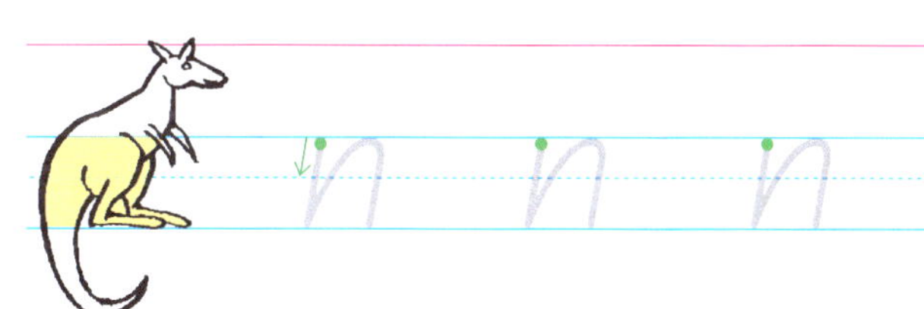

m

Finish the scales on the fish. Start on the green dots.

One, two, three, four, five,
Once I caught a fish alive.
Six, seven, eight, nine, ten,
Then I let it go again.

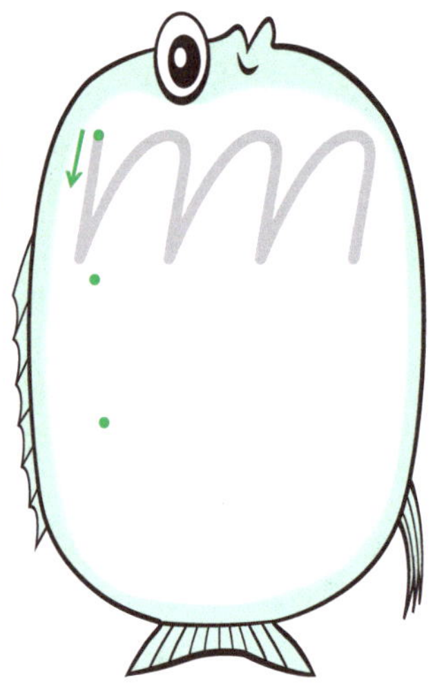

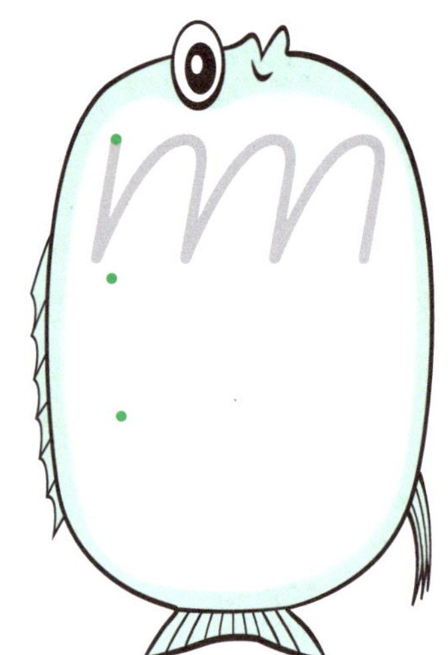

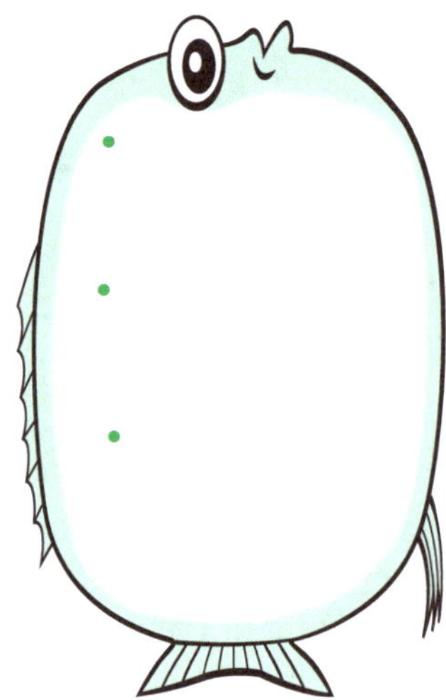

Trace and continue the pattern.

mm mm

Trace and finish the frogs' eyes.

Trace and write m.

m m

Trace and write m.

m m

Trace and continue the pattern.

Draw humps on the camels.

Trace and write m.

Colour.

How many miles to Babylon?
Three score miles and ten.
Can I get there by candlelight?
Yes, and back again.
If your heels are nimble and light,
You may get there by candlelight.

Trace and write m.

r

Draw a spout on each watering can.
Start on the green dots.

Trace and continue the pattern.

Give each flower a stem and a leaf.

Trace and write r.

Trace and write r.

Trace and continue the pattern.

m m

Give the spiders more legs.

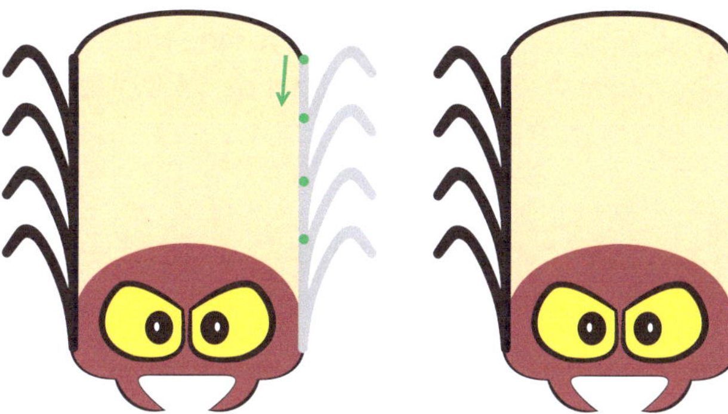

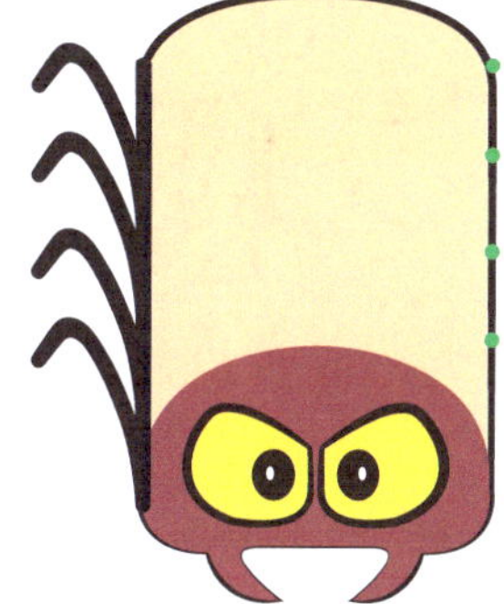

Trace and write r.

r r r

Colour.

Little Miss Muffet
Sat on a tuffet
Eating her curds and whey;
There came a big spider,
Who sat down beside her
And frightened Miss Muffet away.

Trace and write r.

r r r

h

Give the sheep lots of fluffy wool.
Start on the green dots.

Baa, baa, black sheep,
Have you any wool?
Yes, sir, yes, sir,
Three bags full;
One for the master,
And one for the dame,
And one for the little boy
Who lives down the lane.

Trace and continue the pattern.

Draw three bags on each wagon.

Trace and write h.

h h h

Trace and write h.

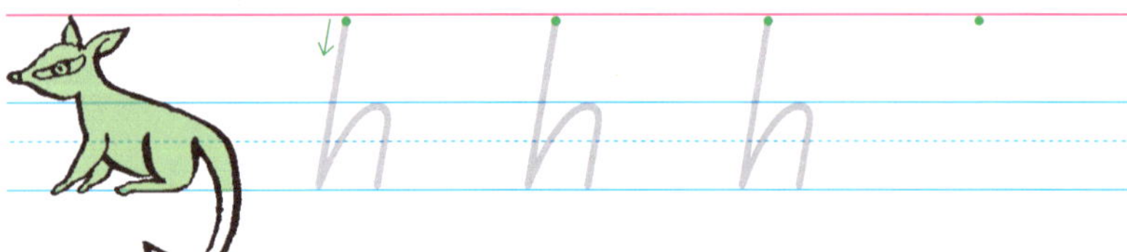

h

I had a little turtle,
I called him Tiny Tim.
I put him in the bathtub
To see if he could swim.

Make a pattern on Tiny Tim's shell.

Trace and write h.

h h h

Add scales to the alligator purse.

Trace and write h.

h h h

k

Give each bird a beak. Start on the green dots.

Sing a song of sixpence,
A pocket full of rye;
Four and twenty blackbirds
Baked in a pie.

Trace and continue the pattern.

Trace and continue the pattern.

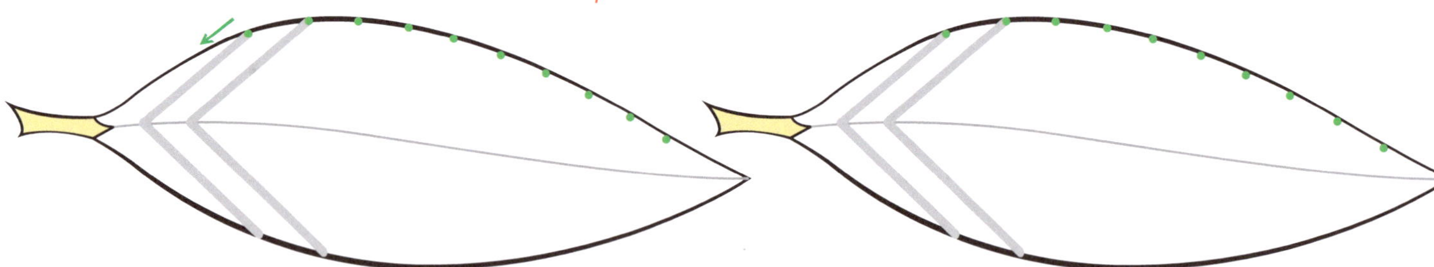

Trace and write k.

k k k

Trace and write k.

k k k

Trace and continue the pattern.

Draw blades on the scissors.

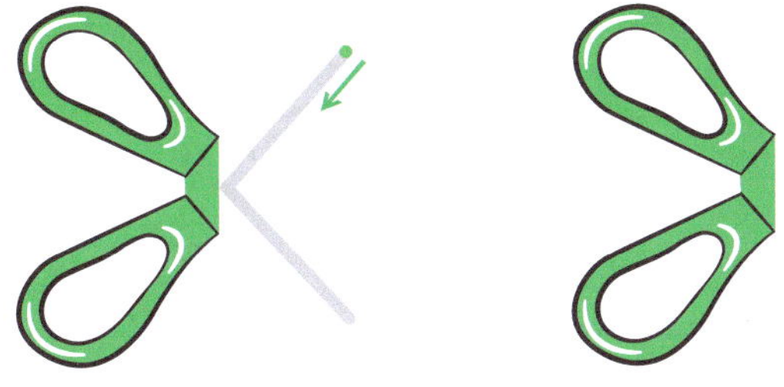

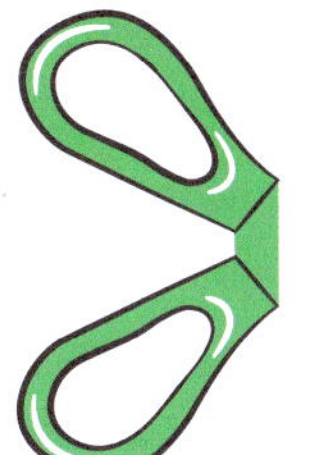

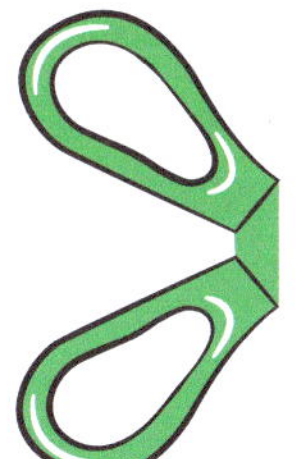

Trace and write k.

Draw more blackbirds. Add washing to the line. Colour.

The maid was in the garden,
Hanging out the clothes,
When along came a blackbird,
And pecked off her nose.

Trace and write k.

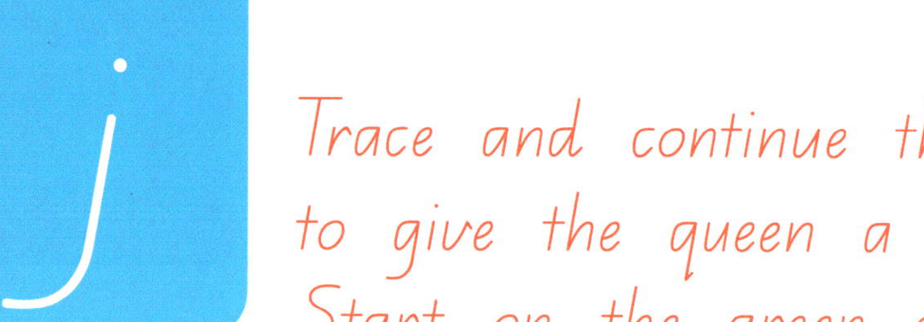

Trace and continue the pattern to give the queen a fringe. Start on the green dots.

Pussy cat, pussy cat, where have you been?
I've been to London to visit the queen.
Pussy cat, pussy cat, what did you there?
I frightened a little mouse under her chair.

Give each mouse a tail.

Trace and write j.

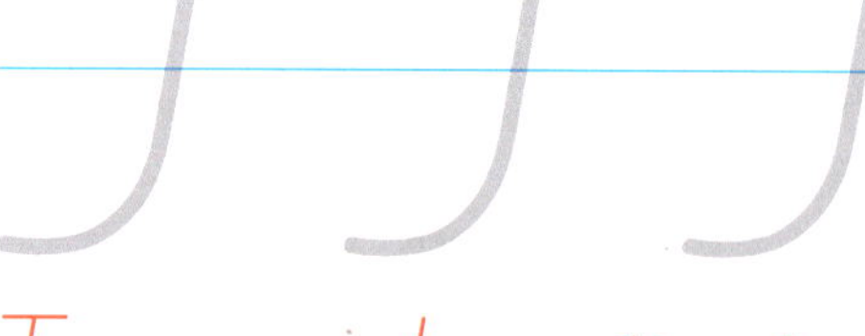

Trace and write j.

j

Give each cat a tail.

Trace and write j.

Give each gingerbread man some buttons. Colour.

Trace and write j.

b

Ladybird, ladybird
Fly away home.

Trace and write b. Start on the green dots.

b b b

Give each ladybird legs.

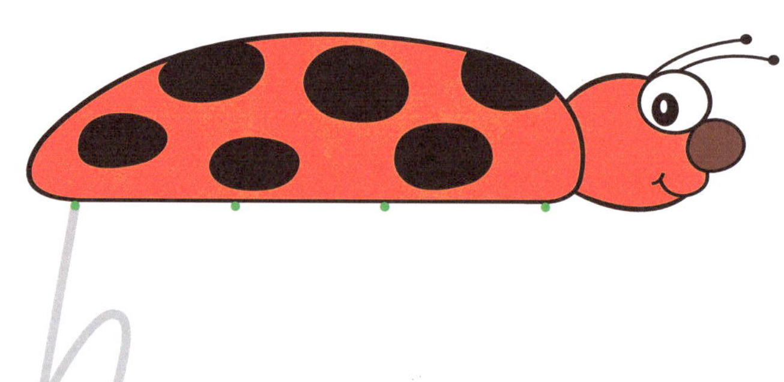

b b

Trace and write b.

b b b

Trace and write b.

b b b

Draw more chickens.

Chook, chook, chook, chook, chook,
Good morning, Mrs Hen.
How many chickens have you got?
Madam, I've got ten.
Four of them are yellow,
And four of them are brown,
And two of them are speckled red,
The nicest in the town.

Give each cup a handle.

Trace and write p.

p p p

Trace and write p.

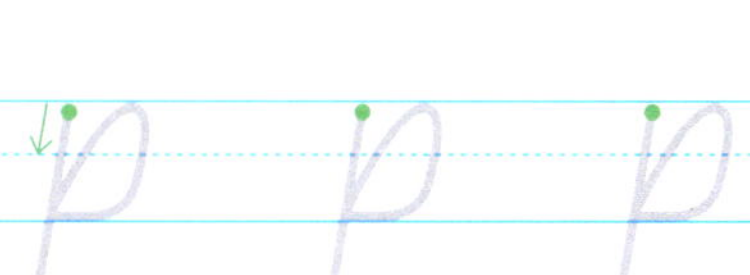

u

Trace the feathers. Add more. Start on the green dots.

The Owl and the Pussy-Cat
Went to sea
In a beautiful pea-green boat;
They took some honey,
And plenty of money
Wrapped up in a five-pound note.

Trace and continue the pattern. Start on the green dots.

Trace and finish the owl's wings.

Trace and write u.

Trace and write u.

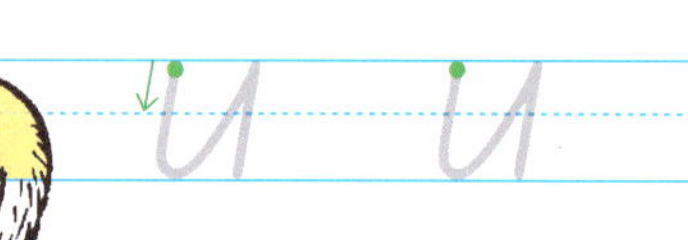

Trace and write the patterns to make each cake.

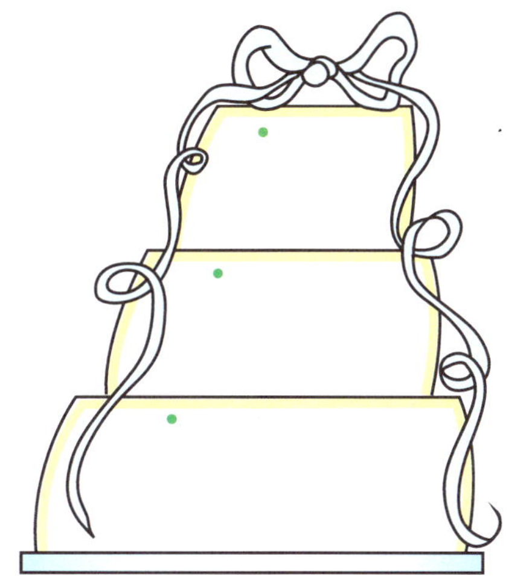

Trace and write u.

u u u

Add more waves. Colour.

What a beautiful
pussy you are, you are,
What a beautiful pussy
you are.

Trace and write u.

u u u

w

Trace then add more tiles to the roof.
Start on the green dots.

There was an old woman who lived in a shoe,
She had so many children she didn't know what to do.
She gave them some soup with fresh, buttered bread
And read them a story and tucked them in bed.

Trace and continue the pattern.

Trace and write w.

Trace and write w.

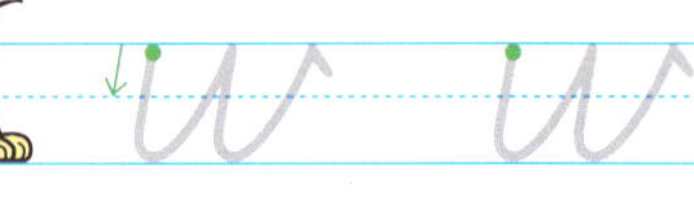

v

Trace the pattern. Add more to the cradle.

Rock-a-bye baby,
On the tree-top,
When the wind blows
The cradle will rock.
When the bough breaks,
The cradle will fall –
Down will come baby,
Cradle and all!

Trace and continue the pattern.

Add v to finish each baby singlet.

Trace and write v.

Trace and write v.

f

Draw an arm on each soldier. Start on the green dots.

The grand old Duke of York,
He had ten thousand men.
He marched them up to the top of the hill
And he marched them down again.
And when they were up they were up,
And when they were down they were down,
And when they were only halfway up,
They were neither up nor down.

Trace and draw bones on the fish.

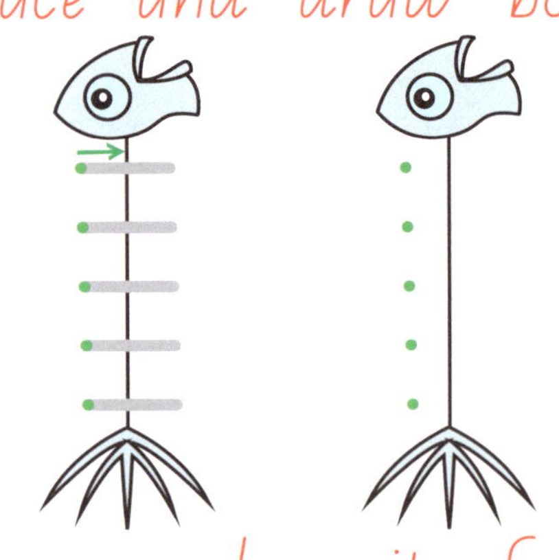

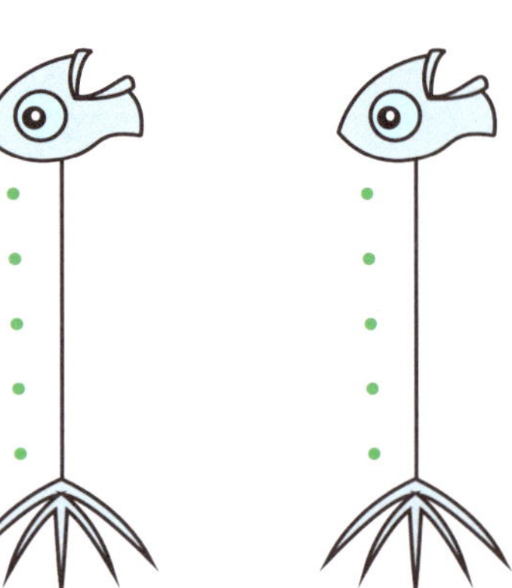

Trace and write f.

Trace and write f.

Trace and draw a tail on each cat.

Trace and write f.

Colour.

I love little pussy,
Her coat is so warm,
And if I don't hurt her
She'll do me no harm.
So I'll not pull her tail,
Nor drive her away,
But pussy and I
Very gently will play.
She shall sit by my side,
And I'll give her some food;
And pussy will love me
Because I am good.

Trace and write f.

a

This little piggy went to market, This little piggy went home.
This little piggy had roast beef, This little piggy had none.
And this little piggy went wee, wee, wee, wee all the way home.

Draw an arm on each pig. Start on the green dots.

Trace and continue the pattern.

Trace and draw five toes using this pattern. Add toenails.

Trace and write a.

a a a

Trace and write a.

a a a

Draw a wing on each bee.

Trace and write a.

a a a

Colour.

Trace and write a.

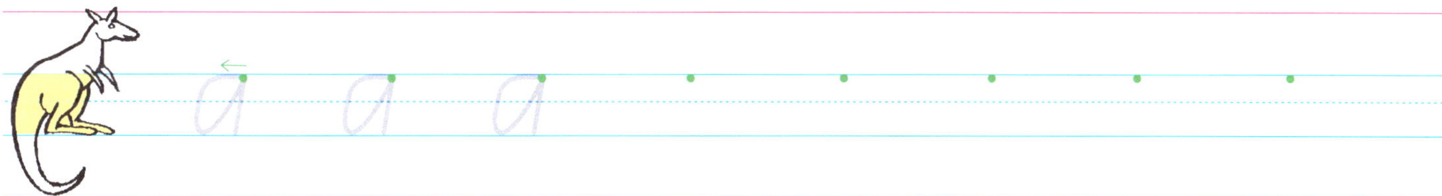

q

Trace and draw more boards on the house.
Start on the green dots.

There was a crooked man
And he walked a crooked mile.
He found a crooked sixpence
Beside a crooked stile.
He bought a crooked cat,
Which caught a crooked mouse,
And they all lived together
In a crooked little house.

Trace and give each man a walking stick.

Trace and write q.

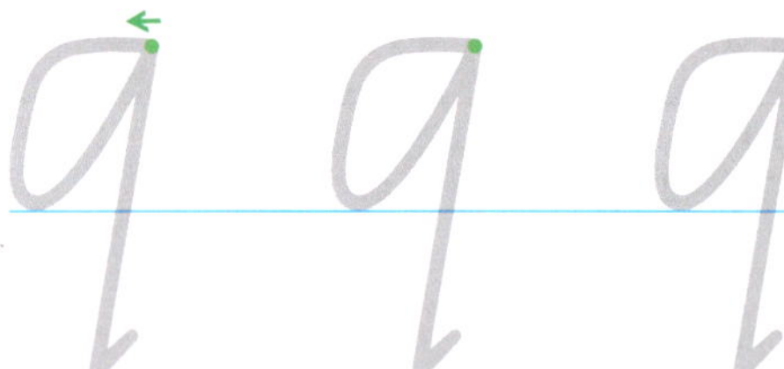

Trace and write q.

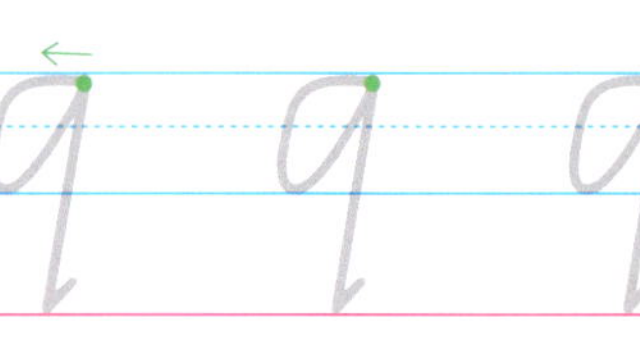

q

Give each bird a wing.

Trace and write q.

q q q

Draw pears on the tree. Colour.

I had a little nut tree,
Nothing would it bear
But a silver nutmeg
And a golden pear;

The King of Spain's daughter
Came to visit me,
All for the sake
Of my little nut tree.

Trace and write q.

q q q

d

Trace the legs and draw more.
Start on the green dots.

I eat leaves for breakfast,
I eat leaves for lunch,
I eat leaves for dinner,
Munch, munch, munch,
munch, crunch.

Trace the fish hooks. Draw more.

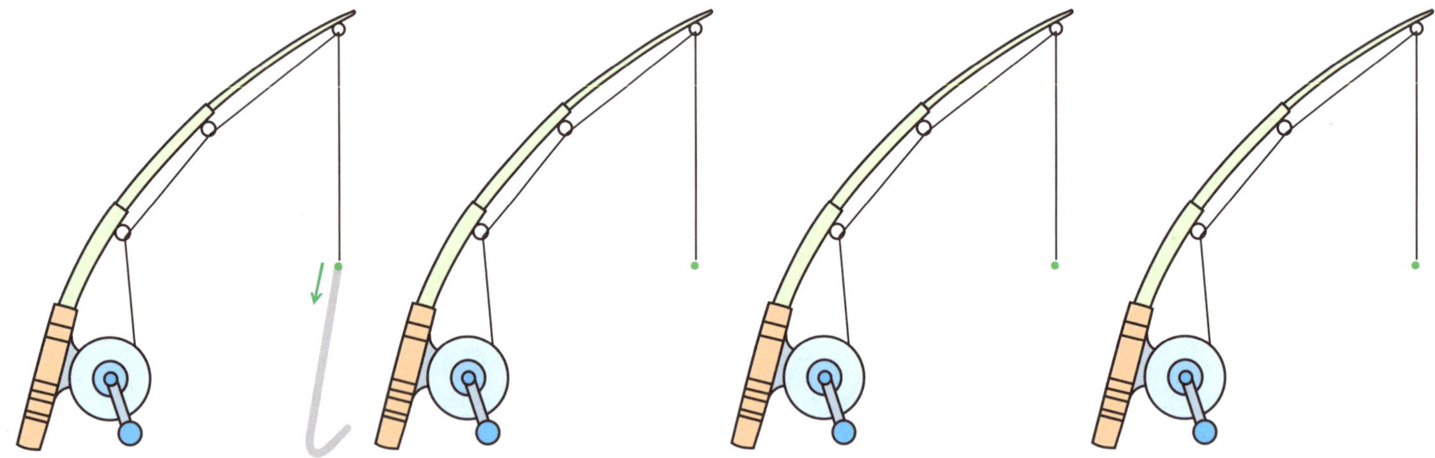

Trace and write d. Start on the green dots.

d d d

Trace and write d.

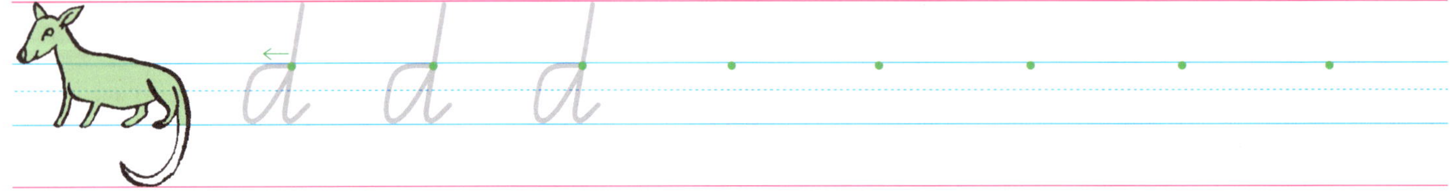

d

Give each butterfly two antennae.

Trace and write d.

d d d

Colour.

How many insects come here and go
In an English country garden?
I'll tell you now of some that I know,
Those I miss you'll surely pardon.
Fireflies, bugs, wasps and bees,
Spiders climbing in the trees,
Butterflies drift in the gentle breeze.
There are snakes and ants that sting,
And other creeping things
In an English country garden.

Trace and write d.

d d d

e

Trace the pattern.
Draw more curls.
Start on the green dots.

Curly Locks, Curly Locks, will you be mine?
You shall not wash dishes, nor yet feed the swine.
You'll sit on a cushion and sew a fine seam,
And feed upon strawberries, sugar and cream.

Trace and continue the pattern.

Draw a curly tail on each pig.

Trace and write e.

Trace and write e.

Trace the pattern. Give each sheep more wool.

Trace and write e.

e e e

Add some sheep.
Colour.

Little Bo Peep has lost her sheep
And doesn't know where to find them.
Leave them alone and they'll come home,
Wagging their tails behind them.

Trace and write e.

c

Trace each c. Add more.
Start on the green dots.

Little Arabella Miller
Found a furry caterpillar,
First it crawled upon her mother,
Then upon her baby brother.
"Oh," said Arabella Miller,
"Take away that caterpillar."

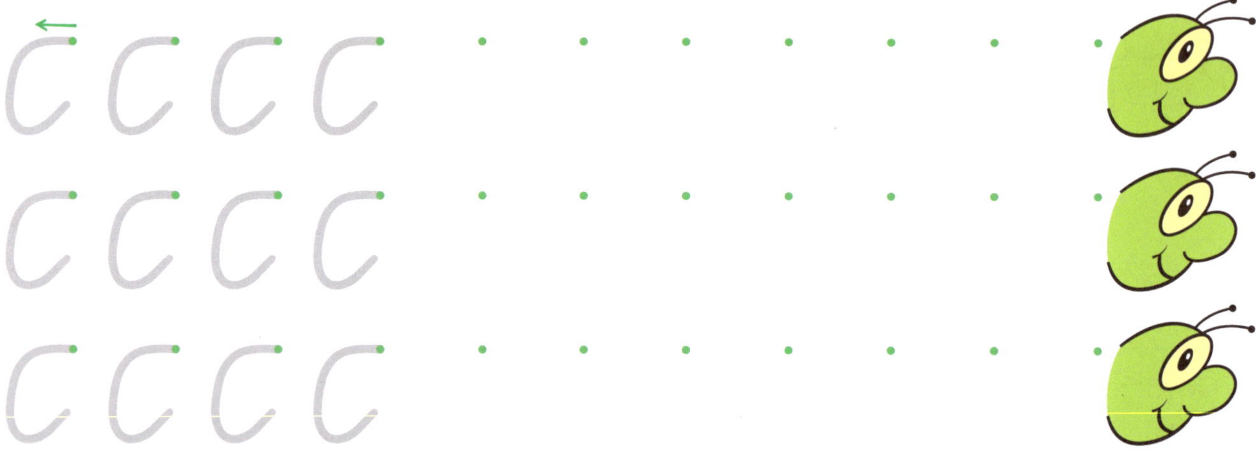

c is shaped like e. Trace the pattern. Write more.

Trace and write c.

Trace and write c.

c

Trace the pattern. Add more.

Draw an ear on each dog.

Trace and write c.

Draw some food in the cupboard. Colour.

Old Mother Hubbard went to the cupboard
To fetch her poor doggy a bone.

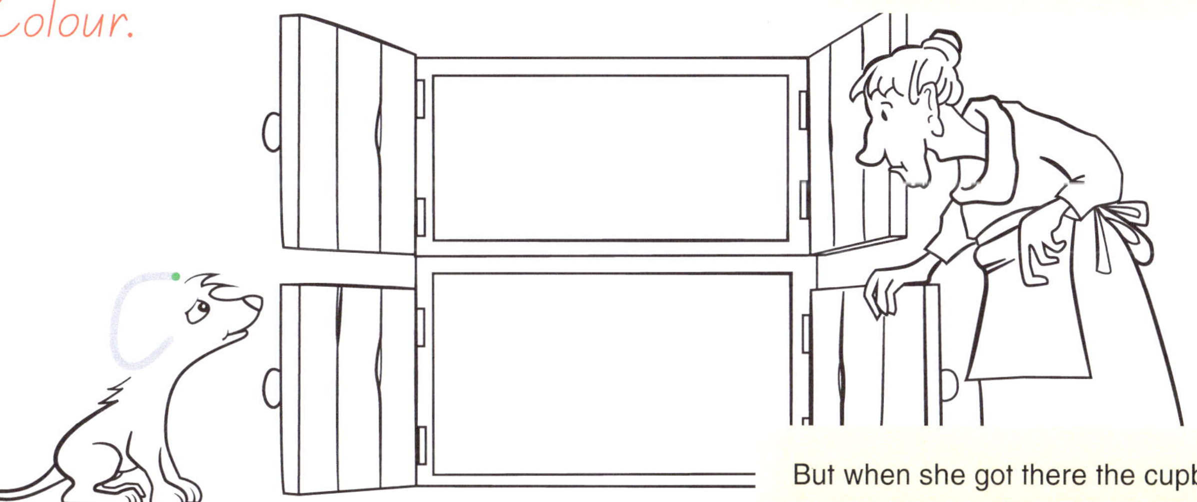

But when she got there the cupboard was bare
And so the poor doggy had none.

Trace and write c.

o

Trace the eggs. Draw more. Start on the green dots.

Hickety, pickety, my black hen,
She lays eggs for gentlemen;
Sometimes nine and sometimes ten,
Hickety, pickety, my black hen.

o is shaped like e. Trace the pattern. Write more.

eee eee

Trace and write o.

o o o

Trace and write o.

o o o

Trace Humpty Dumpty. Draw more.

o

Trace and write o.

o o o

Draw more cherries on the plate. Colour.

One, two, three, four,
Mary at the cottage door,
Five, six, seven, eight,
Eating cherries off a plate.

Trace and write o.

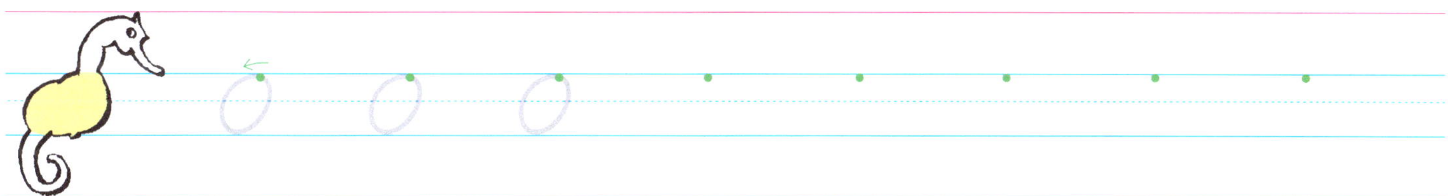

s

Trace each s. Write more to make steam. Start on the green dots.

Polly put the kettle on,
Polly put the kettle on,
Polly put the kettle on,
We'll all have tea.
Sukey take it off again,
Sukey take it off again,
Sukey take it off again,
They've all gone away.

Give each girl a curl.

Trace and write s. Start on the green dots.

Trace and write s.

Give each horse a tail.

Trace and write s.

s s s

Colour.

Horsey, horsey, don't you stop,
Just let your feet go clippety-clop;
Your tail goes swish and the wheels go round,
Giddy-up, you're homeward bound!

Trace and write s.

s s s

y

Trace each tail shape. Draw more to make a shaggy dog. Start on the green dots.

Where, oh where has my little dog gone?
Where, oh where can he be?
With his tail so long
And his ears so short.
Where, oh where can he be?

Trace and continue the pattern.

Trace and write y.

Trace and write y.

Add a tail to each kite.

Trace and write y.

y y y

Add more stars. Colour.

Twinkle, twinkle, little star,
How I wonder what you are.
Up above the world so high,
Like a diamond in the sky.
Twinkle, twinkle, little star,
How I wonder what you are.

Trace and write y.

y y y

g

Draw a g on each ant.
Add more legs.
Start on the green dots.

The ants go marching one by one,
Hoorah, hoorah,
The ants go marching one by one,
Hoorah, hoorah,
The ants go marching one by one,
And the little one stops to beat his drum,
And they all go marching down
To the ground to get out of the rain.

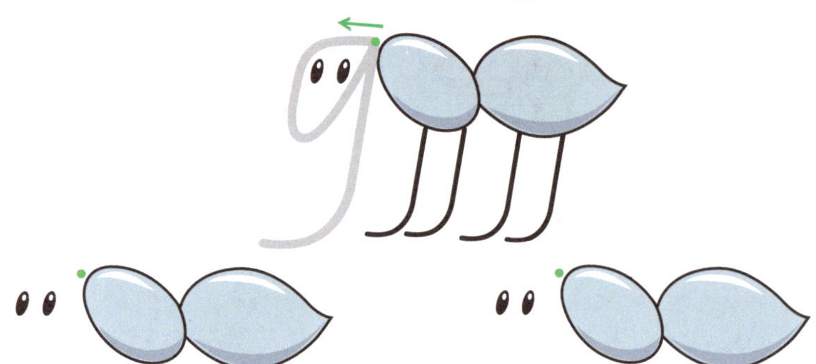

Draw a handle on each umbrella.

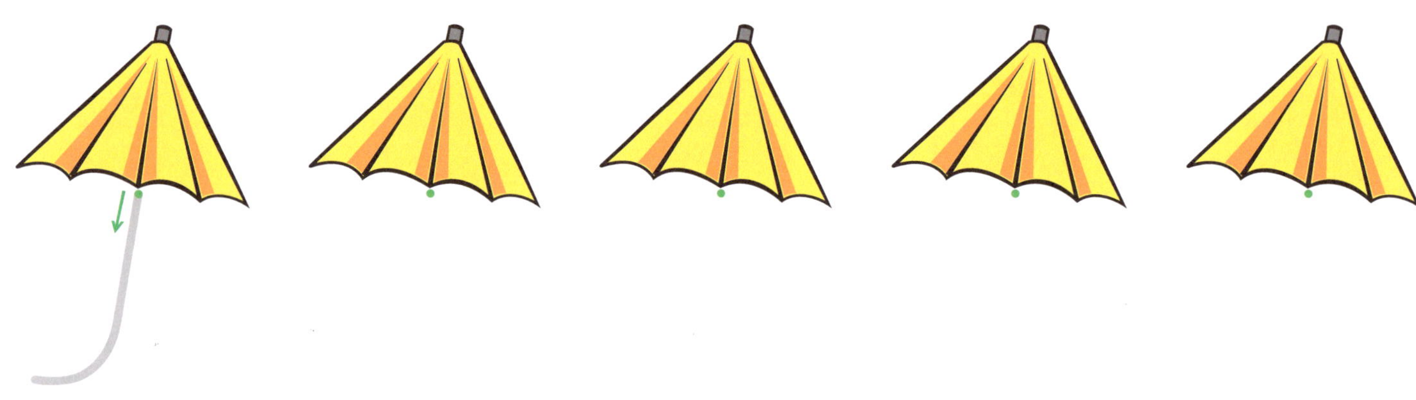

Trace and write g.

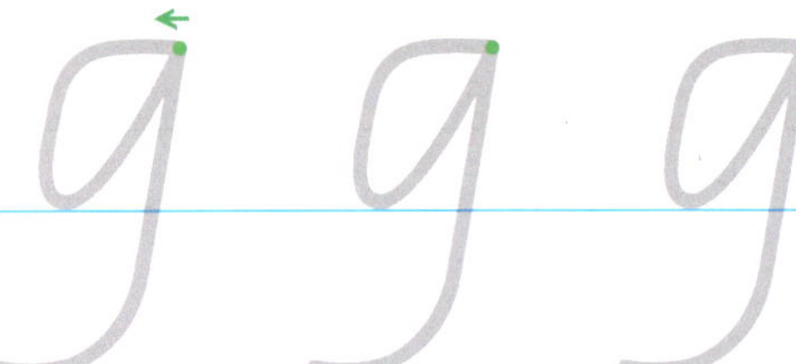

Trace and write g.

g

Draw a robe on each king.

Trace and write g.

g g g

Draw some tarts on the tray. Colour.

The Queen of Hearts
She made some tarts,
All on a summer's day.
The Knave of Hearts
He stole the tarts,
And took them clean away.

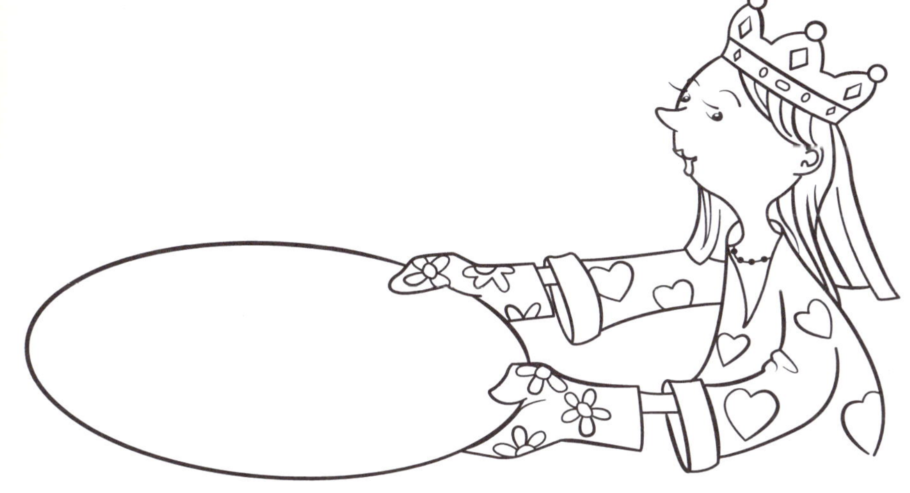

Trace and write g.

g g g

z

Trace each z. Write more. Start on the green dots.

Little Boy Blue
Come blow your horn.
The sheep's in the meadow
The cow's in the corn.
But where is the boy
Who looks after the sheep?
He's under the haystack
Fast asleep.
Will you wake him?
No, not I. For if I do, he's sure to cry.

Trace each line. Draw more.

Trace the ladder. Draw more.

Trace and write z.

Trace and write z.

TEACHER'S NOTES

On all pages green dots for "go" are given as starting points for tracing and pre-writing patterns. Top-to-bottom, left-to-right movements are reinforced, with directional arrows given at the start of every line of work. After relevant pre-writing patterns, each letter is placed on a blue base line. Lastly, each letter is placed on Year One 8 mm red and blue lines for children to try. At the start of each set of 8 mm red and blue lines is an animal figure with the relevant spatial aspects for the letter of the page shaded. The letter types are body, head and body, or body and tail. Slope is developmental and should be talked about and encouraged, but not expected at this early stage.

Page

1 All numerals start at the top of their form. Arrows are given only for numerals requiring two strokes (numbered) or where the direction is not obvious. An "open" eight is shown, as open and closed forms, both acceptable in Qld, commence in the same place.

2 List of contents

3 Introduction

4 Lower-case "i" is a head and body letter.

5 Dot the "i" after writing the downstroke. Dots should be small; "i" is a body letter.

6 Lower-case "t" starts halfway between the top red and top blue lines, making it shorter than "l". It is a head and body letter.

7 As the left-to-right stroke of "x" will be written first in the cursive form, it is essential that this is written first now.

8–21 The clockwise "three-mountain pattern" is useful for developing the rhythm and flow of handwriting. It has been lengthened in some pre-writing patterns to four or more "mountains", but mostly only three as this is ideal for maintaining the correct shape and allowing the hand to move across the page. As all clockwise letters are based on the "three mountain pattern", it may be useful to superimpose the letter being studied over it.

8–9 "n" is a body letter.

10–11 "m" is a body letter with two "mountains".

12–13 "r" is a narrow letter based on the letter "n" shape. It is useful to verbalise "r" as having three movements: down for the "vase", up for the "stem" and "over" for the rosebud; "r" finishes with a rounded, angular downstroke to differentiate it from "v"; "r" is a body letter.

14–15 "h" is like "n", only with a longer downstroke. It is a head and body letter.

16–17 "k" starts like "h" but curves in, then "kicks" out. It is a head and body letter.

18–19 The flat "tails" of letters is the inverse flat "shoulders" of "a" pattern letters; "j" goes under the blue base line and finishes flat along the bottom red line. It does not resemble a curved hook. The dot on "j" is written last and should be small; "j" is a body and tail letter.

20 "b" is written like "h", with the base closed in. It finishes flat like the tail on "j". It is a head and body letter.

21 "p" should be written fluently without a pencil lift. Write the downstroke, then "come back up the pole" to complete the loop of "p" that is shaped like that of "b". It is a body and tail letter.

22–33 The anti-clockwise "three scoop pattern" is also useful for developing the rhythm and flow of handwriting. It has been lengthened in some pre-writing patterns to four or more "scoops", but mostly only three as this is ideal for maintaining the correct shape and allowing the hand to move across the page. As this group of anti-clockwise letters is based on the "three scoop pattern", it can be useful to superimpose the letter being studied over it.

22–23 "u" is a body letter.

24 "w" is a body letter with two scoops. It finishes with a short pointed stroke.

25 "v" is a body letter, also finishing with a short pointed stroke.

26–27 "f" starts with a flat "shoulder" that is the inverse of the flat tail on "j". The second stroke must be left-to-right as this is how it will join in cursive; "f" is a head and body letter.

28–29 "a" is shaped like "u", only it starts with a flat "shoulder". It is a body letter.

30–31 "q" is shaped like "u", with a flat "shoulder" and pointed tail. It is a body and tail letter.

32–33 Only "d" and "e" do not start at the top of their form; "d" starts where "a" starts, then goes up tall, then "back down the pole" without lifting; "d" is a head and body letter. "d" finishes with a tail, or cursive exit, to minimise the "b"–"d" confusion.

34–39 The running writing "e" pattern usually has three loops, but can be longer, as for the "three mountain pattern" and "three scoop pattern". See note for pages 8 to 21.

34–35 Only "d" and "e" do not start at the top of their form; "e" starts in the middle on the dotted blue line. It is a very slim letter; "e" is a body letter.

36–37 "c" is like "e" with a "shoulder", or like part of "a". It starts flat, not curved and is a body letter.

38–39 "o" is elliptical like "e", with the same narrow base. It must be anti-clockwise and must start in the middle at the top, for correct cursive later; "o" does not have a flat "shoulder". It is a body letter.

40–41 "s" starts with a flat "shoulder" like "a", and finishes like the flat "tail" letters or like "b" and "p".

42–43 "y" is like the letter "u" with a flat "tail". It does not finish with a hook; "y" is a body and tail letter.

44–45 "g" is like the letter "a" with a flat "tail". It does not finish with a hook; "g" is a body and tail letter.

46 "z" has a straight zig-zag movement.

47 Teacher's Notes

48 Certificate

Inside back cover — Reference Card—May be detached and contacted to the student's desk.

Congratulations!
has completed
the Prep
handwriting
program.
Teacher:
Date: